F

MW00963018

Learning Tree
1 2 3

Caterpillars

By Hannah E. Glease

Illustrated by Mike Atkinson

CHERRYTREE BOOKS

PROPERTY OF
FULTONVALE SCHOOL

Read this book and see if you can answer the questions at the end. Ask an adult or an older friend to tell you if your answers are right or to help you if you find the questions difficult. Often there is more than one answer to a question.

A Cherrytree Book

Designed and produced by
A S Publishing

First published 1990
by Cherrytree Press Ltd
a subsidiary of
The Chivers Company Ltd
Windsor Bridge Road
Bath, Avon BA2 3AX

Copyright © Cherrytree Press Ltd 1990

British Library Cataloguing in Publication Data
Glease, Hannah E.
    Caterpillars.
    1. Caterpillars
    I. Title II. Atkinson, Michael III. Series
    595.780439

    ISBN 0-7451-5086-1

Printed and bound in Italy by L.E.G.O. s.p.a., Vicenza

All rights reserved. No part of this publication may be
reproduced, stored in a retrieval system, or transmitted, in
any form or by any means without the prior permission in
writing of the publisher, nor be otherwise circulated in any
form of binding or cover other than that in which it is
published and without a similar condition including this
condition being imposed on the subsequent purchaser.

red admiral
butterfly

A caterpillar is a baby butterfly or moth.
When they grow up, the caterpillars in the
picture will be just like the butterfly.

There are many different kinds of butterfly.
This one is called a red admiral.

There are many different kinds of caterpillar.
Each kind will become a different kind of
butterfly or moth.

There are big ones and small ones.

There are fat ones and thin ones.

There are smooth ones and hairy ones.

Hairy caterpillars can harm your skin.
Never pick up a hairy caterpillar.

Caterpillars are not easy to find.
Look for leaves that have been chewed.

Lay a cloth on the ground under a bush.
Shake the bush and caterpillars may drop off
the leaves on to the cloth.

mouth and spinneret

head

segment

spiracle

leg

proleg

A caterpillar's body has lots of segments.
Near its head, there are three pairs of legs.
The stumps on the rest of the body are prolegs.
They are not real legs but they can grip well.

6

looper caterpillar

This caterpillar moves by arching its body.

Caterpillars can make silk in their bodies.
It comes out through a tube called a spinneret.
The silk is very strong.

Caterpillars have strong jaws.
They eat all the time.

puss moth
caterpillar

Caterpillars like to eat leaves.
Other creatures like to eat caterpillars.
Birds and insects eat caterpillars.
So do lizards and little animals like mice and
shrews.

wasps

blackbird

Farmers are pleased that creatures eat the caterpillars.
It stops the caterpillars eating the crops that they have grown.
Caterpillars do a lot of damage to crops.

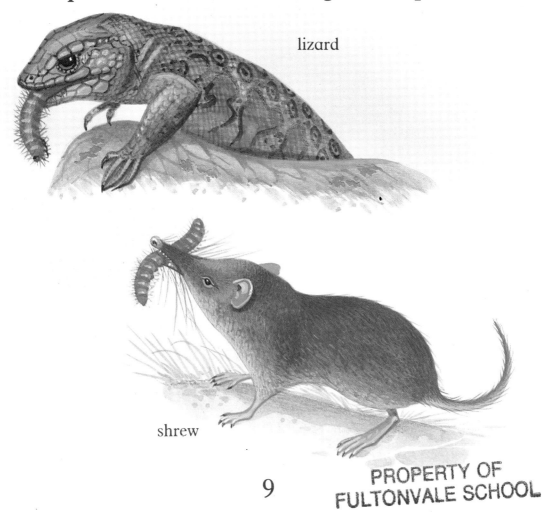

lizard

shrew

9

PROPERTY OF
FULTONVALE SCHOOL

Caterpillars get eaten only if they can be seen.
Some caterpillars are the same colour as the
leaves they feed on.

Other animals cannot see them.

These caterpillars look like twigs.
Can you tell which are twigs and which are
caterpillars?

These caterpillars are poisonous to eat.
Their bright colours warn other animals not to eat them.
Poisonous animals often have bright colours.

cinnabar moth caterpillars

These two caterpillars look very fierce.
They puff themselves up to scare away other animals.

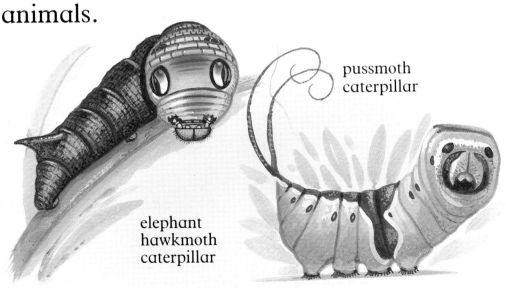

pussmoth caterpillar

elephant hawkmoth caterpillar

A butterfly lays her eggs on a plant.
After a few days tiny caterpillars hatch.

They begin to eat the leaves of the plant.
As they eat, the caterpillars grow fat.
Soon they are too big for their own skins.

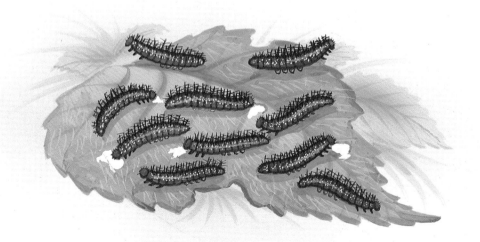

The skins burst and the caterpillars wriggle out.
But the caterpillars have new skin underneath.

After a few weeks, the caterpillars stop eating.
Each one finds a hiding place where it can rest.
It attaches itself to its resting place with silk.

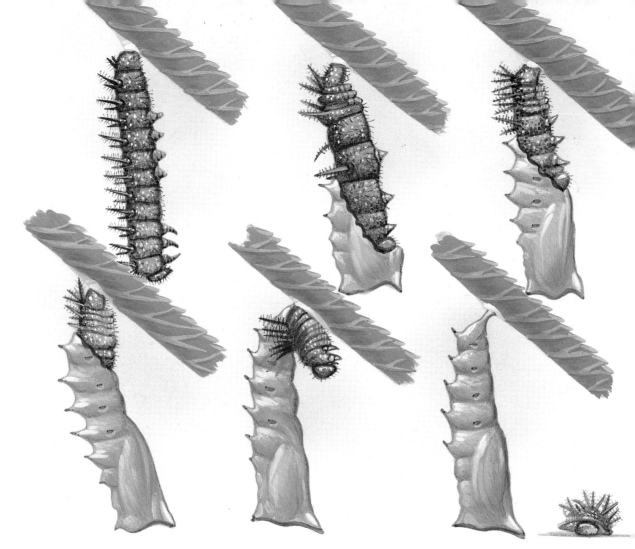

The caterpillar grips the silk with its back legs and hangs from it.
Inside its skin, the caterpillar's body changes into a pupa or chrysalis.

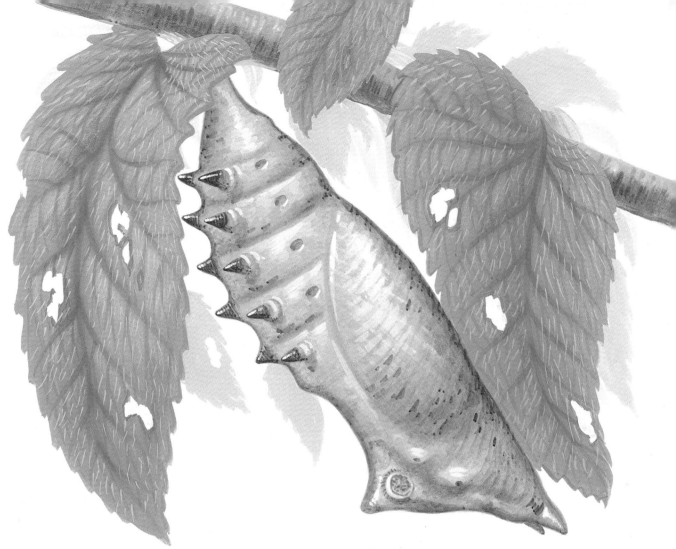

The old skin peels back and falls away.
The chrysalis stays fixed to the resting place.
It does not move and it has no food.
Inside its hard skin, its shape is changing.

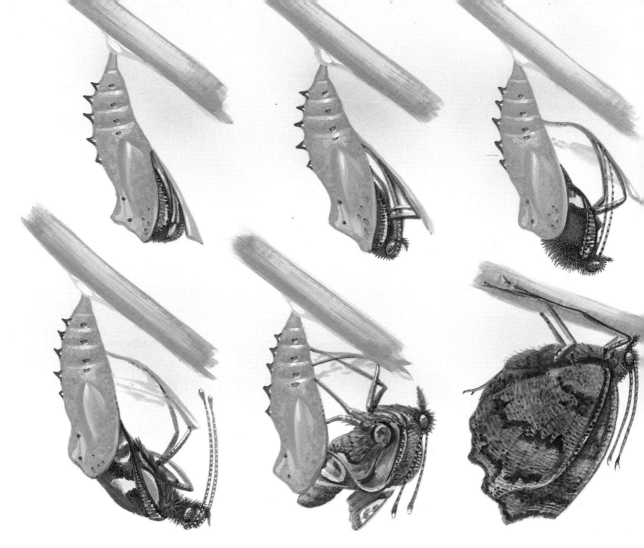

After some weeks or months, the skin splits.
Out comes a head and the top part of a new body.
Then come legs and two wet, crumpled wings.
They belong to a new creature, a butterfly.

The butterfly's body is soft, wet and weak.
But gradually it dries and hardens.
The butterfly spreads its wings and flies away.
It is ready for its first meal of nectar.

You would not guess what beautiful butterflies or moths some dull-looking caterpillars turn into.

Often very colourful caterpillars turn into very dull-looking moths.

clouded yellow
butterfly

scarlet
tiger moth

red admiral
butterfly

Draw pictures of caterpillars that you find.
See if you can find out what the adults look
like and what they are called.
Draw butterflies or moths that you see and
find out about their caterpillars.

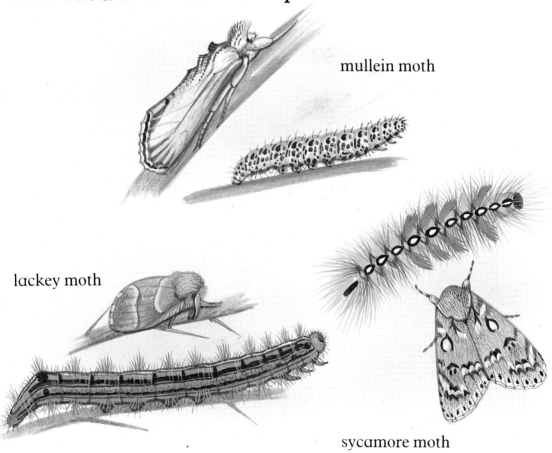

mullein moth

lackey moth

sycamore moth

Make a home for your caterpillars.
You need a big jar or fish tank with a cover, a
jam jar of water and some of the same plants
you found the caterpillars on.
Put in some moss, peat or potting compost.
Many moth caterpillars like to burrow in it to
turn into pupae.

Bring the caterpillars home on their leaves.
They do not like to be picked off them.
Put them in their new home.
Bring them regular supplies of fresh leaves
and watch them turn into butterflies or moths.

More about caterpillars

The four stages in a butterfly or moth's life cycle are: egg, larva (caterpillar), pupa (chrysalis), adult.

Scientists call the change that takes place in the insect's shape metamorphosis. It is a Greek word that means changing shape. The word chrysalis is also Greek. It means golden. Some chrysalis shells shine like gold.

The female butterfly lays between 50 and 1000 eggs. The eggs are often stuck to the plant. Some kinds hatch in a few days, others take months. The first thing they eat is often their own shell.

Caterpillars are like little feeding machines. They eat all the time, but will usually only eat one type of plant. The butterfly always lays her eggs on that type of plant. It is called the food plant.

The larva or caterpillar eats so much that it may shed its skin four or five times.

Caterpillars have eyes on the sides of their body but they can only tell dark from light.

Caterpillars breathe through tiny little holes in their sides called spiracles.

Some caterpillars spin a cocoon of silk round their body when they turn into pupae. The silkworm moth caterpillar is bred for its silk.

Some caterpillars take less than two weeks to turn into butterflies or moths. Some take more than a year.

Caterpillars do enormous damage to crops. The cabbage white butterfly used to be a serious pest. Now farmers use insecticides to kill the caterpillars.

Butterflies are useful creatures. They help to pollinate flowers. If all the caterpillars are killed, there will be no adult butterflies. Many people are now trying to conserve butterflies.

1

1 What kind of an animal is a caterpillar?

2 What does a caterpillar do all day?

3 Do pretty caterpillars turn into pretty butterflies?

4 A butterfly is an insect. Name three other kinds of insect.

5 Can you see the caterpillars in this picture? How does it help a caterpillar not to be seen?

2

6 Why do you think that some butterflies stick their eggs on to the leaves?

7 Try to find three different types of caterpillar. Draw them in colour in your notebook. See if you can find out the name of the adult butterfly or moth. It will not be easy.

8 Name the kind of food plant you found the caterpillars on.

9 Look for butterflies on stinging nettles. See what kinds of butterfly lay their eggs on them. Be careful if you pick the leaves.

10 Make a home for the caterpillars you collect.

11 Why do you need to put a cover on the container?

12 See how long the pupation stage takes for your caterpillars.

22

3

13 Keep a notebook to record what you find out about caterpillars. See how many kinds you can find. Write down where and when you found them, and watch out for the adult butterflies and moths.

14 What use are the cinnabar moth caterpillar's coloured stripes?

15 What does metamorphosis mean?

16 Why is it hard to pick caterpillars off their food plant?

17 What kind of a creature is the silkworm?

18 Why do you think most chrysalises are the same colour as their surroundings?

19 Moths mostly fly at night. They often rest on tree trunks by day. Why do you think it helps them to be dull coloured?

20 What do caterpillars do with the silk they make?

21 How does an elephant hawkmoth caterpillar frighten away birds?

22 Why can't a butterfly fly as soon as it leaves its chrysalis?

23 The looper caterpillar on page 7 does not have as many prolegs as most other caterpillars. Can you think why?

24 Some caterpillars turn into butterflies or moths. What happens to the rest?

25 Caterpillars can mostly eat only their particular food plant. Can you think of a way of helping to conserve caterpillars?

Index